Praise for

OR GET SICK ALONG THE WAY

"Wow – what a great read! This will help a lot of folks figure out how to protect themselves and their families from the consequences of suffering any of the other hazards we face as we get older."

Bill Biordi
Insurance Industry Leader

"Well Done! I love its storytelling combined with facts – sure made me keep reading!"

Kim Butler
Author/Coach, *Live Your Life Insurance*

This book is a good lesson in not procrastinating about important issues we prefer to ignore!

Abram Brustein CLU, ChFC, CLF, MSM
Insurance Industry Leader

With refreshing openness and understanding, the author recounts the final years of his dad's life while teaching us how to evaluate and select the most useful insurance. Once you finish the book, you should know the choices available and how to proceed.

Joshua Barol
Certified Occupational Therapist

Or Get Sick Along The Way

AVOID FINANCIAL DEVASTATION FROM
CRITICAL, CHRONIC, OR TERMINAL
ILLNESS

David Barol

Bala House Publishing
Bala Cynwyd, Pennsylvania

Or Get Sick Along The Way

Copyright © 2014 by David Barol. Revised 2024.

All rights reserved. No part of this publication may be reproduced, distributed, or transmitted in any form or by any means, including photocopying, recording, or other electronic or mechanical methods, without the prior written permission of the publisher, except in the case of brief quotations embodied in critical reviews and certain other noncommercial uses permitted by copyright law. For permission requests, write to the publisher, addressed "Attention: Permissions Coordinator," at the address below.

Bala House Publishing
45 E. City Avenue
Bala Cynwyd, PA 19004
www.BalaHousePublishing.com

Book Layout ©2017 Tugboat designs

Ordering Information:
Special discounts are available on quantity purchases. For details, contact the "Special Sales Department" at the address above or email Info@BalaHousePublishing.com.

Or Get Sick Along The Way / David Barol — 2nd ed.

ISBN 978-0-9914559-6-6

Printed in the USA

Introduction

In your life, you will have three potential outcomes. You will:

- Live too long,
- Die too soon, or
- Get sick along the way.

If you are absolutely, positively sure that you will require long-term care services – and you will need it for a long time – buy Long-Term Care insurance; do it now, for you will not make a wiser purchase.

However, if you are NOT absolutely, positively sure you will need this care or if there is the chance you might suffer a heart attack, stroke, or maybe cancer – or you might die peacefully in your sleep – or get hit by a bus – and you are not one to throw money away, then you should read this book. It couldn't hurt.

Contents

Introduction	v
Which Mistake Will You Make?	1
What's My Story?	5
What is Long-Term Care?	7
The Declaration of Dependence	9
He Who Hesitates	11
What are We Talking About – A Lot of Money?	13
How Will You Prepare For LTC?	17
Life Doesn't Always Turn Out According to Plan	19
Be Careful What You Ask For	22
Deep Dive	25
How It Went Down	50
Peanut Butter Different; Policies Different	52
So I'll Meet 'im Later On	57
Glossary	63
Appendix. What are the Odds?	70
Meet the Author	77

CHAPTER 1

Which Mistake Will You Make?

None of us have a lease on life. No matter how we live or how conscientiously we keep ourselves in shape, something terrible might happen. We could die; we could get sick; we could get injured.

Most of us have not prepared for a life-altering disability or critical illness. We cannot accept something like that happening to us – him, yeah; her, sure, but not me – so we will not spend the time, money, or effort to plan for something we don't want to happen.

But now that you are reading this book. When no one is looking, allow yourself to think about the unthinkable – your infirmity. What do you need to do to protect yourself and your family from the financial consequences of illness, disease, or incapacity? To protect yourself financially means you must save, insure, or invest. When you invest, you put money aside, hoping it will grow to cover whatever needs come your way. If you insure, you pool your money with others, hoping there will be enough to protect you from the unknown. You are sharing the risk with others, so each of you does not have to cover the total cost on your own. This method is less costly, provided each participant does not suffer the same outcome.

This book will pound home the "Small versus the Big Mistake" dilemma. The Small mistake occurs when you insure against a problem that never occurs. The Big Mistake comes when you don't insure but then suffer from the negative outcome, leaving yourself exposed to the financial cost that arises. Let me give you an example.

Last year, while driving to the airport for a European vacation, my wife contacted a company that offers international medical insurance. For $270, she insured both of us for our three-week trip. I felt tired before the trip. In London, pulling our luggage along the street, I felt pressure on my chest. By the time we reached Paris, I couldn't walk three steps without the feeling of a proverbial ice pick stuck in my chest. I went to the American Hospital in Paris (chartered by an act of Congress in 1910). Once they verified my ten-day-old insurance, they checked me in for what turned out to be an angioplasty, a stent, and three nights of relatively good hospital food. My total out-of-pocket cost? Nothing. The insurance even paid for the subsequent pharmaceuticals.

While we were checking in, the French hospital person told my wife about a young American hit by a car while bike riding. He had no travel insurance and received a devastating hospital bill.

My idea of a good time was not suffering pain every time I took a step. The money we spent on the premium could have bought dinner for two in Paris. What if we never used the insurance? Small Mistake versus Big Mistake.

This book will guide you through the options for paying for long-term care services while using real-life examples to drive home the point of how quickly our lives can change.

Just as there is more than one brand of peanut butter, there are many ways to solve this problem. Assuming they all have a place, this book will help you determine the best solution for you. You may get a call from someone pushing one solution over others, as some people walk around with hammers looking for nails. This book will explain, contrast, and compare the various approaches so you can make an educated choice.

Choosing not to protect yourself is also a choice

CHAPTER 2

What's My Story?

Not long after I entered the field of personal finance, my father asked, "Do you know anything about long-term care insurance?"

What do you know? I had just completed a course to become a "Certified Senior Advisor," jamming my brain with so much information it was ready to explode.

"Sure, Dad. I can help."

My father grew up during the Depression and served in World War II and Korea. He was tough, strong, and independent. He reminded me of Jimmy Stewart in *How the West Was Won,* in which his two sons reminisced about how tough he was because he grew up eating buffalo meat.

Although my dad did not grow up eating buffalo meat, the times he lived through made him tough. After tenth grade, he worked on a farm in Vermont to fill in for the young men who had to ship off to fight World War II. He faked his age to enlist in the Navy when he was seventeen. He never complained about his health or lot in life, so the idea that he would ever need to rely on others for his care seemed preposterous. But on the other hand, because of his self-reliance, taking the steps necessary to care for his future made sense. I was determined not to let him down.

CHAPTER 3

What is Long-Term Care?

Before we go on, let's come to terms on some terms.

Long-Term Care (LTC) means helping someone who has lost the ability to independently tend to some of the basic activities of daily living. It is also called *Chronic Care*.

Critical Care. When we suffer a heart attack, we call an ambulance or go to the emergency room, where doctors and nurses will examine and care for us. Our health insurance pays toward the costs of the emergency room, the hospital stay, the cardiologist, and skilled nursing. And then we get better (or we die.)

Activities of Daily Living (ADLs) mark our ability to live independently without needing someone to care for us. Not only can we physically manage these ADLs, but we do not need anyone guiding or directing us to do them.

Activities of Daily Living (ADL's)

Bathing	Continence
Dressing	Transferring
Eating	Toileting

There are plenty of other terms and vocabulary to know, but they got shoved in the Glossary at the end of the book. Plus, I wrote some appendices for those who enjoy probabilities and finance, and I ran through some real-life case studies (after redacting the names as they do in an FBI report).

CHAPTER 4

The Declaration of Dependence

When we were young, we couldn't imagine living a life dependent on others. (Except for when we are young.) The young today are independent of others as they sit around staring at phones paid for by their parents, on sofas bought by their parents, and waiting for dinner prepared by their parents. But they can't imagine being dependent on anyone.

As we move through life, as we get exposed to older people, perhaps even caring for aging parents, we see life differently. Winston Churchill wrote that the best way to die was to get thrown from a horse. There you are, galloping at full speed, and then you are dead a moment later unless you are Christopher Reeve, in which case you will need long-term care.

Most people don't pass quickly from vibrancy to death. Instead, they gradually lose their physical and cognitive abilities. But that doesn't mean it's over. They still enjoy seeing family, reminiscing with friends, reading, listening to music, and finding other comforts in those sunset years of their lives.

Losing physical abilities does not mean our lives are over. And yet, without the extra support from a caregiver, they may as well be. So, in planning for that day, we need to consider the following issues:

· What services might we need;

· Who will provide these services; and

· How we will pay for these services.

Paying for long-term care services for parents, spouses, or themselves reduces people to poverty. Or exhausts them physically or mentally trying to care for someone. Or people don't receive the care they need.

Nobody longs for the day when they can no longer fend for themselves, but this happens. It really does happen.

So, how do we deal with this?

CHAPTER 5

He Who Hesitates

Back to my story.

My dad read an article about the increasing need for long-term care services, which recommended long-term care insurance as the solution. Simple enough. My dad wanted long-term care insurance, and I would help him get it. Here was my plan:

- First, identify quality insurers.
- Next, gather quotes.
- Third, line up one against the other to find the insurance that offers the most benefits for the least premium.

Many's a slip between the cup and the lip.

My dad couldn't meet immediately because he and his wife, not my mother, left for a sailboat cruise around the Greek Islands. We have great pictures of him from that trip, looking like Ernest Hemingway with his close-cropped white beard.

The article that caught my dad's attention showed how the cost of chronic care can ruin a family. But why? What's the big deal about someone helping you get out of bed in the morning?

CHAPTER 6

What are We Talking About – A Lot of Money?

If a home care agency sends someone to your house, they won't send them to stay for ten minutes; they will want them to stay for at least four hours. If the agency charges $25 per hour, but you only need help getting ready in the morning, it will still cost $100.

But your spouse can take care of you; why hire an aid? Sure, any seventy-five-year-old woman can lift her 200-pound (plus) husband out of bed to ensure he bathes and goes to the bathroom. What did "for better or for worse" mean if not that?

Qualified home care agencies provide coverage 24 hours a day and seven days a week. They get paid to hire, train, supervise, and schedule the workers they provide. To provide these workers when you need them, the agency charges a premium over what they pay their staff, so don't figure the person assisting you is making the same as what you are paying.

The best caregivers – the ones who are kind, conscientious, and caring – are rare. After the agency charges its fees, the care worker is lucky to get half. Ask questions about the agencies in your community long before you ever need care.[1] You get what you pay for.

If you require someone to stay all day, say for eight hours at $25 an hour, that comes to $200 a day, $6,000 a month, $72,000 a year. Can your retirement plan handle an additional $72,000 yearly after-tax expenses? The cost of care will vary depending on whether you live in an urban or rural area. If people can find work doing other things, they will, so the cost of these services will depend on the availability of labor.

Wouldn't there be a daily rather than hourly rate? Of course. You will pay less per hour if you pay for someone to stay all 24 hours. But to do that, you must provide that person a place to

---

[1] Like that's going to happen. But it does pay to shop around before you need it. Do yourself a favor.

sleep in a separate room, guarantee at least six uninterrupted hours of sleep, and provide meals. Weekends and holidays, not surprisingly, cost more. So, plan that round-the-clock care will cost $500 a day (in 2022), $1,800 a week, $7,700 a month, and $92,400 a year. Just remember that round-the-clock care in your home is not round-the-clock. If you need 24 hours of care, you must hire someone to fill the gaps.

If you need someone on call 24 hours a day, you must contract waves of people, three or four shifts daily. This is the most expensive care. You would pay the hourly rate times the number of hours. At $25 an hour, that comes to $600 a day, $4,200 a week, and over $200,000 a year.

Annual Cost for Chronic Care	
Home Health Care Aide	$55,000.00
Adult Day Care	$19,000.00
Assisted Living (Private Room)	$51,600.00
Nursing Home (Private Room)	$106,000.00

Genworth Cost of Care Study (2020)

By the time you read this book, the hourly cost may have risen to $50. Just do the math to figure out what one year of long-term care would cost when you need it. For example, if the current cost is $50 an hour, and you figure you will need it in thirty years, then, at an inflation rate of 3%, the cost per hour will grow to $121. And for years inflation for care has grown faster than the rest of the economy.

Since home care becomes prohibitively expensive, you could move to an assisted living facility (ALF) or a nursing home[2]. Nursing homes use more staff per resident than ALFs, which is one reason why they cost more.[3]

These costs are not going down. Although none of us can predict the inflation rate, it is a safe bet; like a fly showing up at a picnic, prices for everything will continue to rise. The cost of chronic care has grown faster than the rest of the economy due to the hands-on nature of this service. As the number of people needing care increases quicker than the number of trained workers who provide it, prices will increase even more.

For many people, LTC means going broke.

---

[2] Another option, while healthy, would be to move to a Continuing Care Retirement Community, but this is not a cost-saving.

[3] From the Met Life study in 2014 for large cities. Other regions will differ. The prices will vary with each year. Bottom line: it's expensive!

CHAPTER 7

How Will You Prepare For LTC?

Big Or Little Mistake?"

Imagine lying on your deathbed, looking over your life. Would you prefer regretting the mistake of paying for long-term care insurance and never using the benefits or not paying for insurance but then needing the care?

Not only can long-term care costs wipe out a family's savings, but the quality of care depends on how much you pay. Having money can spell the difference between living in your home surrounded by family or becoming a ward of a government-run institution.

How shall we pay for long-term care? Let me count the ways:

1. Rely on the mercy of others. Turn your companions into caregivers, making them

pay for your negligence with the quality of their lives.

2. Pay for care out of your diminishing savings until you become so impoverished you qualify for Medicaid.
3. Buy long-term care insurance ("LTCi") while healthy enough to qualify.
4. Qualify for life insurance with a Long-Term Care Rider
5. Buy life insurance with an Accelerated Benefits Rider.
6. Fund an annuity that will double its payout when you need long-term care.
7. Use a Hybrid product to fund long-term care or give your money back if you don't.
8. Move into a Continuing Care Community.

This book will dive into these strategies.

CHAPTER 8

Life Doesn't Always Turn Out According to Plan

The morning after Dad returned from the cruise, he walked outside to get the newspaper. The weather in Philadelphia during January differs somewhat from where he had just been, the Aegean Sea. He was wearing his slippers. They worked. He slipped. Hitting the asphalt hard, he wound up in bed for two weeks.

No, we didn't go over insurance while he lay in bed.

When he got better, he drove into town for a meeting. As a product of the Great Depression, he hated to pay for parking, so he parked on the outskirts of Center City, where he could find a non-metered spot and walk to where he needed to go. He rationalized that he was not only beating the parking lots but getting a workout. On this day, things did not go well. He stopped at every corner to lean against a building. His heart was pounding, and he could not catch his breath.

Dad's doctor smoked cigarettes, was overweight, and panted after any exertion. He retired in December, so fortunately, my Dad already had an appointment with his new doctor. After all, why cause a stir? A few minutes into the physical, the new doctor sent Dad down the hall to see a cardiologist, who wasted no time sending him to the hospital.

When the surgeons opened his chest, they found he had suffered a series of heart attacks over the years, each killing off a piece of his heart. Unlike the liver, which can regenerate, once the cells in the heart are damaged, they never recover. The doctors rearranged his arteries to provide blood and oxygen to the remaining living tissue, and they scraped off the calcification that kept his valves from operating correctly.

Although the doctors deemed the operation a success, he continued to lose strength. On a repeat visit, the doctors detected a tear between the chambers, causing a backflow and reducing the pressure the heart could generate to push the blood around his body. For the next year, he lost color and vitality. The doctors sent him to Boston for another operation, this time inserting something called a "clamshell" into his heart to stop the backflow between the chambers. When he got out of the hospital, he looked three inches taller.

He's coming back!

He began physical rehab to regain his strength, talking glowingly about his workout buddies, women ten to twenty years his senior, but you take what you can get.

But life doesn't always turn out according to the plans we make.

CHAPTER 9

Be Careful What You Ask For

When looking for long-term care services, whether at home or a facility, talk with friends, neighbors, and local agencies on aging to learn about providers in your community. Here are questions to ask that might help guide your search[4]:

- How long has the provider been serving this community?
- Does the agency have any printed brochures describing its services and how much they cost? If so, get one.
- Is the agency an approved provider?
- Is the quality of care certified by a national accrediting body such as the Joint

---

[4] Carol Marak, ElderCare.Gov

Commission for the Accreditation of Healthcare Organizations?

- Does the agency have a license to practice (if required in the state where you live)?
- Does the agency offer seniors a "Patients' Bill of Rights" that describes the rights and responsibilities of the agency and the seniors being cared for?
- Does the agency write a plan of care for the patient (with input from the patients, their doctor, and family) and update the plan as necessary?
- How closely do supervisors oversee care to ensure quality?
- Are agency staff members available around the clock, seven days a week, if necessary?
- Does the agency have a nursing supervisor available to provide on-call assistance 24 hours daily?
- How does the agency ensure patient confidentiality?
- How are agency caregivers hired and trained?

- What is the procedure for resolving problems when they occur, and who can I call with questions or complaints?
- Is there a sliding fee schedule based on the ability to pay, and is financial assistance available to pay for services?
- Will the agency provide a list of references for its caregivers?
- Who does the agency call if the home health care worker cannot come when scheduled?
- What are the types of employee screening?
- What are your costs?

The employees matter most because they will be in your house, moving you in and out of bed, calling on you at night, and treating you like a person or a means to a paycheck.

CHAPTER 10

Deep Dive

Turn your Companions into Caretakers

For most of humanity's existence, parents and children took turns caring for each other. Phenomena such as urbanization, migration, war, famine, and disease disrupted the hierarchical family. Without nearby children and grandchildren, people increasingly turned to professional caregivers.

Trust Me: I Work for the Government

Should you lose the ability to perform the Activities of Daily Living ("ADL") for physical or cognitive reasons, you will not be covered under any governmental program so long as you have the resources to pay for your care. Unlike skilled care, neither health insurance nor

Medicare will cover chronic care costs.[5] You will have to pay these expenses until you have next to nothing, and by next to nothing, I mean one inch above the surface of nothing. Only then can you apply for the government program Medicaid. (See the Glossary for Medicaid qualifications.)

The care under Medicaid differs from the care given to people who can afford to pay for premium services. After all, the meals you can afford on food stamps are not as good as the food you can buy with your American Express card.

If you are married, Medicaid requires you to go through most of your spouse's assets before it kicks in, thus impoverishing your healthy spouse, too. Only then will the government step in and pay for your long-term care.

You may awaken one night with this brilliant thought: "Aha! If I give the kids the money, I can qualify for Medicaid, and then my kids can give me my money on the sly."

---

[5] Medicare will pay for an hour of home care per day a few times a week for the terminally ill under Hospice Care.

That would work except for two slight problems:

a) If you give the kids the money, they will spend it, and

b) the government wasn't born yesterday. It will tally your gifts over the previous five years to determine your Medicaid eligibility. It will delay Medicaid for months or even years to account for those gifts. (You better hope the kids didn't spend the money. Which they did.)

Long-Term Care Insurance

For you, the best time to buy flood insurance is when the hurricane is bearing down. Yet, that's just when those greedy insurance companies won't sell you any insurance. How does that make sense?

The same people must be running the LTC insurance companies because they will reject anyone whose health history suggests they may need long-term care. The insurers look at *morbidity* factors -- the chance of getting sick or injured -- to underwrite their applicants. So, the best time to apply is when you are young and healthy, not when you show your age.

How does Long Term Care Insurance work?

When you trigger two out of the six Activities of Daily Living, you enter the Elimination Period for a pre-set number of days when you need care, but your policy will not pay for it.[6] (You must make sure whether your policy counts days when you receive informal care provided by a non-qualified person, like a family member.) Once you reach the end of the Elimination Period, your policy will either pay you a monthly amount (Indemnity) or reimburse you for qualified expenses (Reimbursement). Most policies will continue these payments until the end of the benefit period. Some policies will go even longer than the benefit period to use up the months in which you did not receive reimbursements for the total amount of coverage[7].

Some LTC policies offer professional care coordinators to help you arrange services and

---

[6] Unless it contains the more costly zero-elimination period.

[7] See Appendix for more details on the probability of using your long-term care insurance benefits.

will pay for home modifications to ensure that you can continue to live at home.

Tax Deductibility of LTC Premiums

Ever since the passage of the HIPPA law in 1997, you may deduct part of your LTC depending on age. The following table shows both the 2022 and 2023 individual limits.

2023 Tax Deductibility

The following table shows the tax-qualified LTC deductible limits per individual (2022 limits in brackets):

Attained Age Before Close of Taxable Year	2023	(2022)
40 or less	$480	($450)
Above 40 but not more than 50	$890	($850)
Above 50 but not more than 60	$1,790	($1,690)
Above 60 but not more than 70	$4,770	($4,510)
Older than 70	$5,960	($5,640)

Despite the actual premium cost, you can deduct only the amount in the table as a health expense on Schedule A of your taxes, and only when your total health expenses surpass 7.5% of your Adjusted Gross Income (AGI), and your total deductions exceed the standard deduction[8].

LTC Through Work

As an employee, your company can deduct LTC premiums without attributing income to you. It gets trickier for owners of sole proprietorships, partnerships, or pass-through corporations who purchase and pay for Tax-Qualified Long-Term Care Insurance policies for themselves, their spouses, and their dependents. They may claim a deduction for the premiums as business medical care expenses[9], provided **the company pays the premium**. The IRS permits partnerships and sole proprietors to deduct the qualified portion of the premiums, leaving the remainder as 1099 income for the owners[10].

---

[8] Consequently, few will qualify to deduct LTC premiums.

[9] (IRC Sec. 162(l)(1)(A) and Sec. 213)

[10] As with all tax matters, verify with your tax professional.

Long-Term Care Partnership

Under Partnership rules, a tax-qualified Long Term Care insurance policy can protect assets from the Medicaid provisions designed to deplete your assets. For example, a $300,000 qualified long-term care benefit will protect $300,000 of assets from the Medicaid spend-down requirement, even if your insurance runs out and you must file for Medicaid.

They Wouldn't Raise Premiums, Would They?

Insurers have increased premiums on existing policyholders despite the initial promise that no matter what happens to your health, they will not raise your rates. Ask anyone with an LTC policy about the annual letter giving the Hobson's choice between accepting a decrease in benefits or an increase in premiums. The companies will tell you they increased the premiums on all policyholders and not on you alone, but that is a small consolation.[11]

---

[11] With more years of experience, the LTC insurance industry, if it survives, will develop a better understanding of long-term care and will not betray the trust of new policyholders as they have existing policyholders.

Summary: LTC Insurance Riders and Benefits

Understand the different riders and benefits before purchasing long-term care insurance:

- Nursing home care
- Assisted living facilities
- In-home care
- Adult daycare
- Return of premium
- Restoration of benefit
- Elimination period
- Benefit period
- Daily amount
- Bucket
- Indemnity versus reimbursement
- Care Advisors
- Home Renovations
- Equipment Benefits

Life Insurance

Life insurance protects your family in case of an untimely death. To encourage responsible behavior, the Sixteenth Amendment exempted life insurance death benefits from income taxation. Since then, clever people have extended this unique benefit to other uses besides death benefits, including two methods of covering long-term care expenses.

Life Insurance with LTC Riders

Life insurance with an LTC rider refers to a life policy with additional coverage for long-term care expenses. This product combines the benefits of life insurance and long-term care insurance, providing policyholders with financial protection for both their end-of-life needs and potential long-term care costs. Here's how this product works:

Life Insurance: At its core, this policy functions as traditional life insurance, paying a death benefit to its beneficiaries upon the insured's passing. The death benefit is typically income tax-free and can be used to cover funeral expenses, outstanding debts, income replacement for dependents, or any other financial needs of the beneficiaries.

Long-Term Care (LTC) Rider: This feature helps policyholders protect their assets and alleviate the financial burden associated with long-term care expenses.

Triggering LTC Benefits: To qualify for the LTC benefits, the policyholder generally needs to meet specific eligibility criteria, such as being unable to perform certain activities of daily living (ADLs) independently or requiring substantial assistance due to cognitive impairment. The exact requirements may vary based on the terms and conditions of the policy.

Payouts: When policyholders qualify for LTC benefits, they receive regular monthly payments of either 2% or 4% of the face amount up to the federal monthly maximum adjusted each year for inflation. This is an indemnity payment, not a reimbursement, so it does not require documentation on LTC expenses.

Impact on Death Benefit: The LTC benefit payouts will reduce the policy's death benefit. The specific reductions depend on the policy terms, the amount accessed for long-term care, and any applicable policy limits.

Flexibility and Customization: Life Insurance with LTC Riders often provides flexibility and customization options. Policyholders can tailor the coverage by choosing the benefit amount, the length of the LTC benefit period, and other policy features. Some policies may offer inflation protection to account for rising long-term care costs.

The terms and features of Life Insurance with LTC Riders can vary among insurance companies. It is crucial to review the policy documentation with an experienced agent or advisor, including the terms, conditions, benefits, and limitations, to fully understand how the policy works and what it covers.

Life Insurance with ABR

An alternate way of covering LTC is by adding an Accelerated Benefits Rider ("ABR"). The ABR pays a discounted portion of the policy face amount (not of the lower cash value) up to the insurance company's limits[12] in cases of chronic, critical, or terminal illness.

Taxation: Generally, amounts paid as accelerated death benefits under a life insurance contract are fully excludable from your gross income, provided the payout relates to the cost of the critical illness or injury. The payouts are entirely tax-free for an insured who is terminally ill[13]. ABRs paid to an individual who is

---

[12] A key difference among insurance companies is the percentage of the death benefit you can accelerate. It is not always 100%.

[13] A terminally ill individual is any individual who has been certified by a physician as having an illness or physical condition that can reasonably be expected to result in death within 24 months of the date of certification.

chronically ill are generally excluded from gross income to the same extent as they would be under a tax qualified LTC insurance policy.

Most of the cost of a critical illness, such as cancer or a heart attack, would be covered by health insurance or Medicare. Nevertheless, you might have to pay an insurance co-pay, or you may need to recover at a care center or lose significant time from work, which is how an ABR can help financially.

After a triggering event (heart attack, stroke, dementia, etc.), you file a claim. The company analyzes your medical records to determine how the triggering event shortened your life expectancy. Since the company expected to pay the death benefit eventually, advancing it while you are alive won't put it out of business. The insurance company will shave off a piece of the distribution, like a slice of cheese, to pay for the lost time value of the money. The company will reduce the payout to accommodate paying you a few years earlier than initially expected when it issued the policy.

Each company offers a variation on this theme. Some will accelerate only the first $500,000 of the death benefit. Others may go as high as the first $2 million. Some may cover ALS; others may not. Some consider terminal illness to mean two years to live, while other insurers restrict this to six months. It pays to read the fine print.

The remaining untouched death benefit will continue along as if nothing happened. The company will not raise the premium on the remaining death benefit despite its newfound knowledge about your health. If anything, the premium will drop since the policy continues with a lower death benefit.

For example, suppose a 50-year-old woman applies for life insurance with ABRs. Based on her gender, tobacco use, predisposition for hang gliding and spelunking -- and let's not forget her voluminous medical records -- the insurance company would come up with a life expectancy: say it figures she would live to age 85. The company will lose money on the deal if she walks out of a coffee shop and gets hit by a bus. But don't lose sleep over the insurance company; it balances her untimely death with people who live beyond expectations. That's why actuaries get the big bucks.

So, let's continue. As this woman reaches for the coffee shop door, she pauses for three seconds to read a flier about a lost cat. As a result, the bus misses her. Twenty years later, at age 70, she suffers a stroke and contacts the insurance company to accelerate her benefit. The insurance company will calculate her new life expectancy.

Suppose the stroke leaves her so incapacitated that her life expectancy drops to three years. In that case, the company will send her a check for part of her death benefit, which it reduces to account for the three-year advance.

Remember what the classically trained economist J. Wellington Wimpy taught us? "I'll gladly pay you Tuesday for a hamburger today," thus teaching generations of elementary school kids the concept of the time value of money, that a dollar today is worth more than a dollar tomorrow.[14]

Insurance actuaries will not pay a whole dollar's worth of death benefit three years before

---

[14] Wimpy was a character in the comic strip Popeye, created by E. C. Segar. Full Disclosure: He wasn't really an economist.

its due date because, at the very least, the company could have earned interest.

If, for example, the insurance company could invest the dollar in a three-year Treasury Note at 5%, then for every $100,000 in death benefit she accelerates, the insurance company would send her a check for $86,384 representing a 14% discount (less a service fee for the expense of collecting and analyzing medical records).

Take away the stroke but add dementia. There is a good chance she will live longer than three years but will need care for the rest of her life. Although her dementia requires guidance to perform at least two of her six ADLs, it did not significantly reduce her life expectancy. In this case, the reduction in death benefit would generate a check for a lesser amount. For example, using the same 5% discount factor, taken over ten years, not three, the company would reduce her benefit by 39%. She would receive $61,000 for every $100,000 of death benefit she accelerates.

This approach encourages people to purchase insurance because they can leave to their heirs what they don't spend on long-term care. Conversely, what they might spend on care will no longer be available for their family. So, figure out what is important to you. Leaving a legacy, maximizing your current spending, or safeguarding against a healthcare event.

Annuities with LTC

Annuities with Long-Term Care (LTC) riders combine the features of annuities with additional coverage for long-term care expenses. An annuity is a financial product designed to provide a guaranteed income stream. By adding an LTC rider, policyholders can access additional funds for long-term care needs. Here's an explanation of annuities with LTC riders and how they generally work:

Annuity Basics: An annuity is a contract between an individual (annuitant) and an insurance company. The annuitant makes a lump sum or a series of premium payments to the insurance company. In return, the insurance company promises to provide a regular income stream to the annuitant immediately or in the future.

LTC Benefit Payouts: An annuity holder can receive additional distributions on top of regular payments when triggering a long-term care event. The amount and duration of the LTC benefits will depend on the annuity contract terms and the specific rider.

Impact on Annuity Benefits: LTC benefits will reduce the annuity's accumulated value and, consequently, any money left for the beneficiaries. (But if you want to leave money to heirs, use life insurance; the purpose of an annuity is to provide an income you can never outlive.)

Flexibility and Customization: Annuities with LTC riders may offer customization options. Policyholders can typically choose the amount of LTC benefit coverage, the duration of the LTC benefit payments, and other features based on their needs and preferences. Some annuity products may also provide inflation protection for rising long-term care costs.

Tax Considerations: The tax treatment of annuities with LTC riders may vary depending on the specific product and jurisdiction. Generally, the LTC benefits from the annuity may be tax-free if used to pay for qualified long-term care expenses. However, any remaining annuity distributions may be subject to tax. (An annuity consists of two types of money: the principal and the gain. The IRS does not tax the principal if paid with after-tax dollars. It taxes the gain as ordinary income.)

Annuity terms and features will differ among insurance companies and products. Therefore, work with an experienced advisor to help you carefully review the policy documentation, including the terms, conditions, benefits, and limitations, to understand how the specific annuity with an LTC rider works and what it covers.

Hybridization

There is a new insurance concept to encourage people to protect themselves. Using either life insurance or an annuity as a base, the product allows you to add money to an account that will provide you with a tax-free multiple of your premium to pay for long-term care insurance or a death benefit in case you never trigger long-term care. This differs from the life and annuity options mentioned earlier because it provides a more considerable LTC benefit for the premium.

You can make a single deposit or pay periodically into this product, which will provide a death benefit, money available for you to take out for emergencies, or if you change your mind and walk away with some of your money, and tax-free payments if you need long-term care. The policy makes more money available for long-term care than for the death benefit or the surrender value. The joint protection rider allows you to cover two lives under the same policy.

Tax-free Benefits: You will pay no income tax if you use this product for qualified long-term care expenses (subject to IRS monthly maximums.) Moreover, the IRS will not charge income tax on whatever passes to your beneficiaries at death.

Deductibility of Premiums: The premiums are split between life and long-term care. The LTC portion qualifies for the health deduction on Schedule A of your taxes or as a business expense. (Life insurance premiums are not tax deductible.)

Looking Under the Hood: The product consists of a modified whole life that pays no dividends. The whole life policy requires level premiums, which either you or an attached annuity pays. In case of a triggering event, the life insurance will pay a monthly amount of up to 100% of the face amount of the policy. After

using up the life insurance value, the product continues paying as a long-term care policy.
1. **Long-Term Care Benefit Payments:**
   a. (AOB) Acceleration of Benefits – pays from the original life insurance face amount.
   b. (COB) Continuation of Benefits – the company continues to pay for the selected period.
2. **Coverage for Long-Term Care Services:** The Hybrid product typically covers various types of care, such as nursing home care, assisted living facilities, in-home care, adult daycare, and other qualified long-term care services. The specific services covered may vary based on the policy details.
3. **Benefit Triggers:** A medical professional must state that the policyholder can no longer perform two ADLs independently.
4. **Benefit Period and Coverage Options:** These policies offer different benefit periods, such as 25 months, 50 months, or for life.
5. **Elimination Period:** The elimination period is the waiting period that policyholders must satisfy before they

become eligible for benefits. It will be up to the policyholder to cover the cost of care during this time. The policies offer various elimination periods, such as ninety days for facility care and zero days for home health care.

6. **Premiums:** The cost will depend on various factors, including the individual's age, health status, desired benefit period, elimination period, and coverage amount. Applicants can pay monthly, quarterly, semi-annually, or annually over specified periods such as 10, 20, or to age 95. Or the applicant can make a single premium payment. Premium sources could include cash, a 1035 exchange from an existing life policy, or an IRA, provided the applicant understands the IRS will tax the premium as an IRA withdrawal.

7. **Inflation Protection:** This is optional, but it can increase the monthly benefit amounts by a percentage to keep pace with inflation over a set number of years, for example, by 5% over twenty years.

8. **Other Customization Options:** Customization options might include shared care benefits for couples, return of

premium, additional premiums during the first six months, or additional riders for enhanced coverage.

Life Plan Communities

Continuing Care Retirement Communities (CCRCs), often called Life Plan Communities, are residential retirement communities that offer a range of housing options and care services to seniors as they age. The primary feature of CCRCs is that they provide a continuum of care, allowing residents to transition between different levels of care as their healthcare needs progress from independent living to skilled nursing care.

Here are the key components and features of CCRCs:

Independent Living: CCRCs typically begin with independent living units for active and healthy seniors. Residents in independent living have private residences (apartments, cottages, or villas) and enjoy amenities such as communal dining, fitness facilities, social activities, transportation services, and pickleball.

Assisted Living: As residents age and require assistance with activities of daily living

(ADLs) like bathing, dressing, or medication management, they can move to an assisted living apartment within the same community. Assisted living provides support while allowing residents to maintain independence.

Skilled Nursing Care: CCRCs often include on-site skilled nursing facilities or nursing homes. These facilities are equipped to provide 24/7 medical care and support for residents with more advanced healthcare needs, including those recovering from surgery or managing chronic conditions.

Memory Care: Some CCRCs also have specialized memory care units for residents with Alzheimer's disease or other forms of dementia. These units offer a secure environment and specialized care tailored to the needs of individuals with memory impairments.

Continuum of Care: The primary advantage of CCRCs is the ability to transition between these different levels of care without needing to move to a different facility. Residents can stay within the same community and receive the appropriate level of care as their health status changes.

Entry Fee and Monthly Fees: CCRCs typically require residents to pay an entry fee upon admission, which can be substantial. Additionally, there are ongoing monthly fees that cover various services and amenities. These fees can vary widely depending on the community and the specific level of care.

Contract Types: CCRCs may offer different contract types, such as life care contracts (all-inclusive) or fee-for-service contracts (pay-as-you-go). The contract type affects how much you pay and what services are included.

Financial Planning: Due to the significant financial commitment associated with CCRCs, individuals considering moving to one should carefully review their financial situation and consult a financial advisor to ensure they can comfortably afford the fees.

Choosing the right CCRC requires careful consideration of individual needs, financial resources, and the specific services and amenities each community offers. Visit and thoroughly research different CCRCs to find the one that best aligns with your lifestyle and healthcare preferences as you age. You will want to do this several years before you consider moving to one, as there are often waiting lists at the better places, and you will want to move in before your health declines.

Mutual Exclusivity: Purchasing life insurance, annuities, or other options does not conflict with moving into a CCRC. Life insurance and annuities offer death benefits or life income, so they deliver money according to their primary purpose, regardless of later conditions. Even the hybrid policies do not conflict with CCRCs since they can provide money when one's health triggers the ADLs regardless of where you live.

CHAPTER 11

How it Went Down

A year after his heart operation, Dad's doctors discovered a tumor growing in his colon. He went under the knife again, but this time he did not bounce back. Whether it was the cancer or the operation, he was never the same. Instead of the man who could move (and climb) mountains[15], these critical illnesses left him pale, weak, and tired.

He moved to an apartment in a Continuing Care Retirement Community, selling the house that gave him so many years of pleasure and saying goodbye to the gardens he so lovingly tended. He and my stepmother decorated their two rooms to resemble their living room and bedroom, including several bookcases that

---

[15] We grew up with a walking stick he used to climb Mt. Fuji while serving in Japan during the Korean War.

housed his "museum" of shells, fossils, and antiquities he collected on his travels.

After a few months, the doctors fitted him with an Implantable Cardioverter Defibrillator (ICD) to restart his heart if it should stop. In January, he said, "I don't know what's going on with this damn thing; it went off sixteen times over the weekend."

I said, "Dad, if it's not working, tell the doctor you need it replaced. You shouldn't have to put up with some piece of junk."

My dad often quoted the Navy phrase: "There's always the ten percent that never gets the word."

At the end of March, he moved from the apartment into the nursing facility because he needed help with the Activities of Daily Living. He slept most of the day and needed help getting out of bed. Most of my visits were spent reading while he slept. A few days later, he died.

He was only 76, but during the last seven years of his life, like a ship floundering against the rocky shoals, his body was battered by one *critical event* after another.

CHAPTER 12

Peanut Butter Different; Policies Different

HOW DO THESE DIFFERENT PRODUCTS COMPARE?

When an insurance company underwrites a policy with an ABR, it looks at the likelihood of dying. LTC insurance underwriters may reject people with Multiple Sclerosis, arthritis, or even an old skiing injury because they underwrite for morbidity. Companies do not underwrite for annuities. People can receive life insurance policies with conditions that would cause a company to reject them for LTC insurance.

The Big Difference

The most significant difference is that long-term care insurance only has *a chance of paying* a benefit. In contrast, none of us avoids death; to put it more sensitively, life insurance will pay

100% of the time.[16] When you have life insurance, you will always leave money behind. Almost all life insurance has a chronic care rider. If it does not, you will pay for LTC out of pocket and continue to pay the life insurance premiums. You will deplete your savings but leave a death benefit. With life insurance, you can pay toward your care without depleting your other assets while still leaving a partial death benefit for your surviving spouse and your family.

Some people will not buy long-term care insurance because they don't want to pay premiums and receive nothing. The LTC riders on life insurance and the Hybrid policies guard against the cost of chronic care without worrying about throwing away the premium.

"Insurance You Don't Have to Die to Use"

---

[16] See Appendix for more details on the probability of using your long term care insurance benefits.

Hybrid vs LTC

Both hybrid products and traditional LTC insurance aim to cover the costs of long-term care expenses. However, they go about it differently, like two separate paths heading to the same destination.

A hybrid insurance product combines elements of life insurance and LTC coverage. You pay premiums, and if you need long-term care, the policy provides you with a pool of money for those expenses. If you don't need long-term care, the policy provides a death benefit to your beneficiaries. It's like having a financial safety net for your care and your loved ones' future.

Traditional LTC insurance is more straightforward. You pay premiums specifically for long-term care coverage. If you require long-term care, the policy covers those expenses. It's a dedicated policy for that purpose.

Here's where they differ:

Flexibility: The hybrid provides more flexibility because it combines life insurance and LTC benefits. If you never need LTC, your premiums aren't wasted because your beneficiaries still get a payout, but not as much as they would from life insurance with an ABR or LTC rider. Traditional LTC insurance pays only if you need long-term care (although there are LTC policies that will return unused premiums.)

Cost: The hybrid might cost more upfront because it bundles two types of coverage. LTC insurance might be more affordable if you only want LTC coverage. However, the lifetime cost of the hybrid will be less because you are assured of receiving money back, one way or the other. Moreover, once you lock in a cost for the hybrid, it will not increase, whereas many people experience rate increases for their LTC insurance.

Benefits: The Hybrid product offers two pools of money. The first is funded with the premium. The second continues the monthly benefits once the premium and the life insurance portion are depleted. Because of this, the Hybrid product provides more LTC coverage than life insurance with the LTC rider given the same premium.

Underwriting: The underwriting process for the Hybrid product differs from LTC insurance due to the combination of life insurance and LTC coverage, emphasizing mortality more than traditional LTC insurance.

Choosing between the different product concepts, LTC insurance, Life with ABR or LTC riders, or Hybrid, depends on your financial situation, goals, and preferences. The Hybrid might be a good fit for a broader financial safety net, whereas LTC was designed to cover specific expenses.

Ultimately, consulting with a financial advisor or independent insurance expert will help you evaluate your needs and select which option best aligns with your plans.

CHAPTER 13

So I'll Meet 'im Later On

At the place where 'e is gone --
Where it's always double drill and no canteen;
'E'll be squattin' on the coals
Givin' drink to poor damned souls,
An' I'll get a swig in hell from Gunga Din!
Yes, Din! Din! Din!
You Lazarushian-leather Gunga Din!
Though I've belted you and flayed you,
By the livin' Gawd that made you,
You're a better man than I am, Gunga Din!

Rudyard Kipling

After my dad died, I thought about that long-term care policy he never purchased. Suppose I brought the application to him as he lay in bed after his slip and fall. Maybe I could have jammed it through the insurance company before the next heart attack. For many years, that is what I thought.

I realize now that he would have paid all those LTC insurance premiums but never received a dime. He would have been further ahead, stuffing those premium dollars into a pillowcase. You see, long-term care (only) insurance:

· Does not pay when you suffer a critical illness like a heart attack or cancer.

· Does not pay for terminal illness.

· Does not pay for nursing care when you stay in a nursing facility for three days.

· And it most definitely does pay when you die in your sleep.

Although he could have bought LTC insurance, in retrospect, only a product with some type of life insurance and one that would pay for a critical or terminal illness -- or death -- would have outperformed the premium pillowcase.

My father died in his sleep during the early hours of April 1, 2004. I visited him twice on that last day of March and kissed his forehead goodbye one last time the next morning. There is rarely a day I don't think about him.

I have known people who got older, taken sick, and died. Some owned long-term care insurance policies and others didn't. The following examples are not data science but just anecdotal. The common thread is except for the peace of mind they may have felt knowing they were covered they would have done better stuffing their premium dollars into a pillowcase.

Would They have Received Benefits?

One woman could not qualify for long-term care insurance because she was a bit short for her weight and suffered from bad knees. (Coincidence?) During the last two years of her life, she developed dementia, requiring exhausting and expensive care. Her family eventually took her to a memory care center, where she died. Had she owned an LTC policy with even a two-year benefit, the family would have saved money, but she waited too long to apply.

Another woman had too many health issues to qualify for LTCi. She stopped working in her early sixties, spending what little money she had accumulated. Since she was on Medicaid by the time her dementia took over, she paid no more money out of pocket, and, of course, she had no money to leave behind. Paying for an LTC policy meant she would have run out of assets sooner than she did, winding up on Medicaid either way.

The Woman Who Knew Too Much

Another woman refused to follow the recommendation of her financial adviser, saying long-term care insurance is a waste of money. She suffered a wasting liver disease that caused her to spend her final seventy days in a nursing facility. Perhaps she was right. If she bought a typical LTC policy with a 90-day elimination period, she would have died before the policy began paying. Moreover, Medicare covers intensive care at the nursing center.

The Man Who Got Something Back

This man paid $78,000 for his LTC insurance policy but dropped it after the company raised his premium every two years. Because the policy contained a Restoration of Benefits feature, he was entitled to receive up to the premium he paid as a benefit. He needed three days of care costing $750 before he died. The company paid $230, citing its $110-a-day limit on home care. He would have been $78,520 ahead using the pillowcase option.

Not One But Two LTC Policies

His wife paid for two LTC policies with zero-day elimination periods, lifetime benefits, and $250-a-day coverage but no cost-of-living adjustments. Although she was diagnosed with pancreatic cancer before Thanksgiving, she did not need long-term care until the end of March. After that, she swiftly declined, requiring three 8-hour shifts of in-home care, which cost $600 daily, more than her combined daily benefit of $500. She paid over $100,000 in premiums for these two long-term care policies but lived long enough to receive just $11,000 in benefits. Chalk up another win for the pillowcase. One of the insurers sent her a letter raising her LTC insurance premiums even though she had already filed a claim. She died before the policy increase went into effect.

Besides the chronic illness, each person suffered at least one critical illness: a heart attack, cancer, or stroke. Had they purchased a life insurance policy that accelerated the benefit for critical illness, they could have received some financial benefit while alive, and they would have left the remaining death benefit to their beneficiaries. Or, if they purchased the hybrid product, they could have used the benefit for long-term care but, if not, returned more than what they put into it to their families.

These are just one person's reflections on death and dying. Nevertheless, all these people, including my dad, could have bought the types of insurance that covered their critical or chronic illnesses while paying their beneficiaries any unused money after their deaths. Knowing they would not waste their money may have encouraged them to do something because if they suffered from dementia or another chronic illness for a long time, each of them could have run out of money.

Glossary

Activities of Daily Living ("ADLs")

- Bathing – washing in either a tub or shower, including getting into or out of the tub or shower.

- Dressing – putting on or taking off all clothing items and any necessary braces or other medical devices.

- Toileting – getting on or off the toilet and performing associated personal hygiene.

- Transferring – moving onto or out of a bed, chair, or wheelchair.

- Continence – the ability to maintain control of bowel and bladder functions; when unable to maintain control, the ability to perform the associated personal hygiene (including caring for catheter or colostomy bag).

- Eating – feeding oneself by getting food into the body from a receptacle (such as a plate) or feeding tube, or intravenously.

Acceleration of Benefits (AOB) Rider

The monthly benefit of a hybrid policy consists of the face amount divided by a selected number of months used to reimburse LTC expenses.

Assisted Living Facility (ALF)

A housing facility for people with disabilities. An ALF provides supervision or assistance with the Activities of Daily Living. It coordinates benefits with insurers and Medicaid and outside service providers while being accountable for its residents' health, safety, and well-being. Although there is no legal definition of the number of residents per care provider, it usually has a larger number than would be in a nursing home.

Chronic Care

The care provided to someone who has been certified by a licensed health care practitioner with a chronic illness that will permanently require assistance in performing at least two Activities of Daily Living, whether for physical or cognitive reasons for at least ninety days.

Comprehensive Care

Some long-term care policies offer home health care only or nursing care only coverage. Although this will reduce the premium, it could limit your options so much that it could make the policy a waste of money, whereas a comprehensive policy will offer care in all settings.

Critical Illnesses

Some companies offer a more extensive list than others because they do not also offer a chronic care trigger. For example, some would argue it is not necessary to include Amyotrophic Lateral Sclerosis (ALS) as a critical illness since it will soon lead to chronic care. Here are examples of triggers used in various policies:

- Major Heart Attack
- Minor Heart Attack
- Coronary Artery Bypass
- Heart Surgery
- Stroke
- Invasive Cancer
- AIDS
- Permanent neurological deficit

- Blood Cancers: Leukemia, Lymphoma, and Myeloma
- End Stage Renal Failure
- Major Organ Transplant
- Paralysis
- Aneurysms
- Loss of Limbs
- Blindness
- Alzheimer's or Dementia
- Coma
  - ALS or Lou Gehrig's disease
  - Severe Burns

Elimination Period

The time between a triggering event and when the insurer pays benefits. Policyholders must have the means to pay for the services during this time. This is the "deductible" for long term care and disability policies. Some policies may require, for example, a ninety-day elimination period for facility care, but zero-day for home health care.

Long Term Care

The care required by a person suffering from a Chronic Illness. (See Chronic Care.)

Medicaid

To qualify for Medicaid, the spouse in question, the "facility spouse," may not possess more than $2,000 in Countable Assets, and the non-facility spouse, the community spouse, may not have assets exceeding $148,620 as of 2023. When the facility spouse has spent her assets – when she has become impoverished – her family can apply for Medicaid, the federal/state program designed to provide care to people with chronic illnesses in poverty. (Medicaid also provides a range of health services to people who are either blind or disabled.[17])

There is also an income restriction, but if the healthcare expenses reduce the participant below the income level, then Medicaid will pick up the extra expense.

Medicaid provides an unlimited number of days at a nursing facility or at home with qualified care. Each state has certain differences

---

[17] "There but for the grace of God go I." The social compact in a society is that we care for each other, as each one of us shares the risk of needing care of some sort. For those of us who want a higher level of care, we can pool our risk and resources through insurance.

in the way it administers the program. After the death of the Medicaid recipient, the state must seek reimbursement of its expenditures by confiscating the assets that were not counted on the front end.

Nursing Home

A residential facility for people who require continual nursing care and have difficulty coping with the ADLs. Nursing aides and skilled nurses are available 24 hours a day.

Terminal Illness

An illness for which a medical professional determines the patient has less than six months or a year, depending on the state, left to live.

Triggering Event

An event written into a contract that leads to the payment of a benefit. It is the inability to perform physically or cognitively at least two ADLs. For the Critical Illness trigger, it is the presence of one of the listed critical illnesses. These events will require verification, usually from a medical professional.

Waiting Period

The time between the purchase of a policy and the time of the first claim. Incidents that occur during the waiting period are not claimable.

Waiver of Premium

A clause in an insurance policy that waives the policyholder's obligation to pay any further premiums should he or she trigger the benefits. Some policies require an extra charge for this rider.

APPENDIX

What are the Odds?

As you know, the financial profession does not deal with run-of-the-mill outcomes but rather risk-adjusted outcomes[18]. When an advisor compares investment A with investment B, she will not show the average returns – that would be misleading. You would expect to see the variation around those returns. "Sure, it averaged 8%, but how many years did it lose money?" This is why an advisor would show risk-adjusted returns.

Comparing Benefits

We calculate long-term care benefits based on many considerations:

- Benefit dollars per day,

---

18 Well, maybe you didn't know that.

- Number of benefit days,
- Elimination period, and
- Cost of Living inflator.

The shorter the elimination period and the longer the benefit period, the more expensive the policy. The compound inflation rider could double the cost of the base policy, but without one, the benefit loses ground each year to inflation.

The total benefit can be misleading when compared to other types of insurance. Assume it would cost $170 daily for an Assisted Living Facility in your area. You may recall that your mother lived five years needing care, so you want an LTC policy paying for five years with an inflation rider, but that costs a lot of money.

One way to save money would be to extend the elimination period from 90 to 180 days. The benefit would start at $170 x 365 days x 5 years = $310,200 and increase with inflation. But is it worth $310,200 when you would have to live five and a half years to collect it all?

So, is $310,200 the Expected Benefit?

You will not receive any benefits unless you trigger the claim, cover the costs of care for the first six months, and then live five years beyond the 180-day elimination period. Your total benefit is $310,200, but that is not the expected outcome, not by a long shot.

$170 per Day

Length of Claim	Potential Benefit
1 Year + 180 Days	$62,000
2 Year + 180 Days	$124,100
3 Year + 180 Days	$186,100
4 Year + 180 Days	$248,200
5 Year + 180 Days	$310,200

What are the odds? There are no hard and fast data, so we must hunt for information and piece it together. This is not an exact science.

According to statistics posted on the Administration on Aging website,[19] there is about a 70% chance that a person reaching age 65 will need some type of care. This would include someone who comes home from the

---

19 http://www.aoa.gov

hospital and needs dressings changed for a week. Of those people, about 40% will need substantial care, meaning they would not be able to perform at least two of the activities necessary for independent living. That comes to 28% of all people reaching age 65.

Many of these people who need substantial care will receive it due to a medical necessity, in which case Medicare would pay for the care. This usually happens after a critical illness.

According to the American Association for Long-Term Care Insurance,[20] presumably an advocate for this type of insurance, the probability of triggering the policy is less than 50%, assuming a zero-day elimination period. The probability of triggering a policy with a 90-day elimination period is less than 35%.[21]

These are statistics drawn from LTC policy owners and not from the general population, not all of whom could qualify for long-term care insurance. People who buy LTC insurance are

---

20 http://www.aaltci.org/long-term-care-insurance/learning-center/probability-long-term-care.php

21 This means that 30% of the policy owners died in the first three months after triggering the ADLs.

less at risk than people who cannot purchase long-term care insurance.[22]

Many who need care will need less than thirty days of it. The 28% figure slips to 20% for those needing care for 90 days and less than that for those needing care for 180 days.

Of people needing care, only 20% of those will need it for five years (the others will die.)

So where does that leave us? Forty percent of 70% is 28%. Of those, less than 20% will need care long enough to meet a 90-day deductible. Of those, only a fifth will live five years needing chronic care. So that brings the odds down to 3% to 6% of those reaching 65. Add the lengthy elimination period, and the percentage of those using the entire LTC insurance benefit drops even more.

The Expected Benefit

If the potential benefit is $310,000, but the odds of ever receiving that money is 3.0%, then

---

[22] They must be healthy enough to qualify – no football injuries, no diabetes, not too overweight, etc.

the expected value is $9,000.[23] How much will the premiums cost for this policy? How is that for a rate of return?

There are a lot of generalizations that have gone into this calculation, for example, this data is based on an existing population of people needing care, not on people who are now considering the purchase of insurance, who may be in better or worse shape than their predecessors.

If you win the long-term care lottery and need care for an extended time, you will not care about the odds and statistics. You will be grateful you spent the money to protect yourself and your family. That is the purpose of insurance: to protect against the unknown and unknowable.

Given what you now know, what would you do to protect yourself if you should one day "Get Sick Along the Way"?

---

[23] Actually, it is higher, but the math is far more complicated. We would have to total the probabilities of triggering one month of disability, two months of disability and so forth to get it theoretically exact. But who cares? Increase this expected benefit by one hundred percent and the point would still be the same.

ABOUT THE AUTHOR

David Barol is the author of *Dema: A New Hope: Speaking the Truth about Israel, The Development of Egyptian Nationalism, Live Too Long, Die Too Soon*, and the *Notes from the Trail* series. For more information about David and his work, visit www.keyams.net.

www.ingramcontent.com/pod-product-compliance
Lightning Source LLC
Chambersburg PA
CBHW050444010526
44118CB00013B/1673